CURTIS INTERNATIONAL
PORTRAITS OF GREATNESS

•

General Editor
Dr. Enzo Orlandi

Text by
Giancarlo Buzzi

Translator
Ben Johnson

Published by
ARNOLDO MONDADORI EDITORE
and
THE CURTIS PUBLISHING COMPANY

THE
LIFE
&
TIMES
OF

PETER THE GREAT

CP

CURTIS BOOKS
A division of
The Curtis Publishing Company
Philadelphia • New York

EARLY RUSSIA: AN ORIENTAL DESPOTISM

Until the end of the 17th century, Russia was little more than a semi-barbaric Oriental despotism. Centuries of domination by the Mongol khans and, before that, close economic and cultural dependence upon Byzantium had frozen the Russian mind and spirit in an Eastern mold. Moscow, the capital of the czars, was hardly more than a cluster of ramshackle villages raising its cupolas bravely among the dense forests.

A new spirit, however, seized Russia with the founding of St. Petersburg in 1703. In a short time, this backward giant awoke to take its place among the modern nations of the West. This dramatic change was accomplished by one of the most dynamic and strong-willed rulers of all times, Peter the Great. The history of his reign is the story of a man whose ways were as shocking as they were impressive, but whose personality and reforms left a stamp upon Russia, and history, that has never been effaced.

Russian life centered
around religion, and the
czars devoted much time to
praising God through
architecture. Among the most
celebrated of Moscow's many
churches is the Cathedral of Vasily
the Blessed, within the Kremlin
walls, shown in the photograph
on the opposite page, and above,
in a watercolor by Giacomo
Quarenghi. Quarenghi was one
of a group of Italian architects,
including Rodolfo ("Aristotle")
Fioravanti, P. A. Solari,
Aloisio Novi and Marco Ruffo,
who played a major part in
transforming the Kremlin.
The prints show the Czarina
(opposite page) and a Palm
Sunday procession (left).

5

Traveling in Russia was an arduous undertaking, especially during the spring thaw, when pedestrians and even horses found the deep mud very heavy going. It was better in the winter, when sleighs could be used (as shown in the print above) on the frozen surfaces. The sleighs were actually small, transportable houses, fully provisioned, and complete with doors and windows. One of the great inconveniences of travel was the absence of inns or stations for changing horses on the road. Between cities, there were only smoky, foul-smelling peasant dwellings in which travelers could sleep and refresh themselves. Right: a new czar kisses the icon on his accession to the throne.

Below: Cathedral Square in the Kremlin, in a watercolor by Quarenghi; beside it, a photograph of the square today. The Kremlin, with its imposing buildings, contrasted vividly with the rest of the city. Even the nobility lived in hovels, with benches or wooden tables for beds. Bottom of page: a 17th-century *flogging scene. Floggings were common in ancient Russia. The czars had noblemen beaten, and they in turn punished serfs and peasants in this cruel way. Flogging was used to extract confessions and even to punish schoolchildren. Twenty lashes of the knout were enough to kill a man.*

A BOISTEROUS CAPITAL

Beside the Moscow River stood the outskirts of the 17th-century capital, where the lower classes lived; closer to the center were the homes of the boyars (nobles) and merchants, and the one decent hotel, run by a Frenchman. The houses were usually wooden and highly flammable. The roads were broad, but deep with mud, with planks occasionally laid across them for pedestrians' use. The numerous taverns were always crowded: the Muscovites were heroic drinkers. The grand prince, who controlled the sale of vodka, beer and all other alcoholic beverages, grew rich on this custom, although he also trafficked in salt, wheat, iron, pitch, caviar and furs. Public baths, a setting for utter promiscuity, rivaled the churches in number. In the center of the city, where each street was devoted to a different trade, relative decorum prevailed. But the commercial district was still lively, teeming with merchants, charlatans, artisans, soldiers. Beyond it was the Kremlin, a vast complex of streets, buildings and monuments in a curious mixture of Byzantine and Italian styles. Here stood the residences of the czar and the patriarch of the Church, guarded by the *strieltsy*, a privileged corps of armed guards.

THE ROMANOVS: A NEW DYNASTY

The 16th-century struggle between Russia's two principal cities, Novgorod and Moscow, had ended in the triumph of Moscow and left the other important centers, still recovering from Mongol, Polish and Lithuanian invasions, in decidedly secondary positions. Muscovite autocratic rule soon destroyed all hope for the old communal institutions. The grand princes of Muscovy who, with the accession of Ivan IV ("the Terrible"), assumed the title of "Czar of all the Russias," were ignorant and reactionary; moreover, they took over a land whose society, politics, government and institutions were mired down in inaction and traditionalism. Serfdom, which bound the peasants inescapably to landed estates, had destroyed the only source of autonomous life, the rural community. There were some attempts at progress: Ivan IV, Boris Godunov and the False Dmitri, all gifted with a measure of farsightedness, sought to improve general conditions. But their efforts were thwarted by the laziness of the populace on the one hand and the opposition of the clergy and the boyars, or great nobles, on the other.

Following Dmitri's death came a period of struggle and anarchy, justly known as the "Time of the Troubles." In January, 1613, a *zemsky sobor*, or territorial assembly, met in Moscow to choose a ruler. Conservatives and radicals compromised by elevating Michael Romanov to the throne: a new dynasty had begun. Michael, who was 16 at the time, was such an obscure choice that the delegation sent to offer him the crown actually had trouble locating him. He may have been chosen precisely because of his insignificance. Yet he became the first czar in a line destined to continue for three centuries.

The country Michael took over was a shambles. In 1619, he made his father, the patriarch Philaret, his co-czar. Philaret ruled as a fully empowered sovereign, ably supporting his weak son, until his death in 1633. Michael was succeeded in 1645 by his son Alexis; the latter's son was to reign as Peter the Great. The dynasty, still in its infancy in the middle of the 17th century, began to strengthen its hold on the Russian throne.

Above: Michael Romanov (1596–1645); he shared the throne with his father, the patriarch Philaret. The two strove to bring order to a chaotic Russia, to lay at least the foundations for administrative and tax reforms, and to encourage the settlement of the land. Right: a nobleman in typical 17th-century dress. The nobility as a class was far less important than the clergy.

Left: a 16th-century icon, now in the Louvre. Such religious pictures were objects of veneration, considered sacred in themselves by the Eastern Church. Below: an archbishop and an archimandrite, typical dignitaries of the powerful Russian clergy.

Left: Czar Alexis Mikhailovich and Natalia Naryshkina, Peter's parents. Alexis, a cultured, mild-mannered man, made up for his lack of vigor by his talent for choosing able associates—a quality rare in reigning monarchs. Despite a number of serious uprisings, his reign saw several important developments: a legal code which became the basis for Russian law; reforms in the Orthodox Church under Patriarch Nikon; and the annexation of the Ukraine. Above: Peter as a child.

A DISPUTED SUCCESSION

Peter was born on May 30, 1672, to Alexis Mikhailovich and his second wife, Natalia Naryshkina. When Czar Alexis died at the age of 47, he was succeeded by a child of his first marriage: Fedor II, Peter's half-brother. Fedor's death, after a 6-year reign, precipitated a bitter and bloody power struggle between the families of Alexis' two wives. The Miloslavsky faction, opposed to Peter's succession, was headed by his dynamic half-sister, Sophia.

Since no law of succession existed, Peter's supporters appealed to the people. With the help of the patriarch and the Duma, a kind of House of Lords, Peter was elected czar, at the age of 10. But Sophia and her party incited the powerful *strieltsy* against the boy and his mother. The guard revolted, raged murderously through the palace and, after much bloodshed, succeeded in instating Peter's half-brother Ivan as his co-czar, with Sophia as regent.

Opposite page, above: a commemorative medallion struck on the birth of Peter, and a print showing the three brothers—Fedor, Ivan and the infant Peter—with the patriarch Adrian and the metropolitan. Below: a dramatic moment during the revolt of the strieltsy in 1682. Natalia is protecting Peter from the fury of the rebels who have overrun the palace. Peter never forgot the slaughter of many friends and relatives, the looting and atrocities, and above all the part played in these events by his half-sister Sophia and the Miloslavskys.

EUROPE IN MINIATURE

There were many foreigners in Moscow. They came from Britain, the Low Countries, Switzerland, Poland and Germany. The German group was the largest. The first to settle permanently in the country were technicians brought in by Czar Ivan III. Over the years their numbers had gradually grown, thanks in part to the many soldiers imported by Ivan the Terrible. By Peter's time they numbered in the thousands. All foreigners lived in a part of the capital known as the *nemetskaia sloboda* (German village), a miniature Europe, with a variety of peoples and customs.

These foreigners were far from representing the flower of their native lands. Life in Moscow had few amenities and little charm, which meant that those who decided to settle there were largely drifters, men who were failures in their own countries. There were, however, some men of keen intelligence and strong personality: doctors, apothecaries and engineers who had something to offer Russian society, at least its more open-minded upper classes. But the lower classes mistrusted the foreigners, considering them dangerous unbelievers whose very presence was a menace to tradition and to the purity of their Orthodox faith. This mistrust was so strong that even an enlightened, easygoing and pro-Western czar like Alexis had to prohibit their living outside their own section of Moscow and to forbid them to wear Russian clothes. These measures hurt only Russia, by delaying its exposure to the modern ideas of the West. Meanwhile, the Europeans were a vigorous and dynamic island of activity in a stagnant backwater. The Russians employed their services, but never fully profited from their presence. It is understandable how so restless a young man as Peter found in the *sloboda* escape from the boredom of the Kremlin. There he made his first friends, some of whom were to remain close to him throughout his life, influencing his character and ideas.

On this page: Peter as a child in the sloboda (*left*); as a young man (*center left*); and, sharing a double throne with his half-brother Ivan, receiving a foreign delegation (*directly below*). Ivan (*lower left*) was mentally retarded. He was a czar in name only until his death in 1696: the only evidence that he ever reigned is his name on official documents. In 1684, Sophia married him off to a beautiful girl of noble rank. *Lower right*: an engraving of grain warehouses along the walls of the so-called Chinese City in Moscow.

DISSOLUTE COMPANIONS AND A BRIDE

In the old print on the opposite page, and below, in an 18th-century engraving: the young Peter playing soldier. It was play only up to a point; his games enabled him to organize the nucleus of the regular regiments that later became his personal bodyguard. Uniforms, arms and training were all "according to the book," as in any real militia: Peter even had his first wooden cannon replaced with iron ones. Below, center and bottom: two convivial scenes from the sloboda. *The foreigners' settlement opened a marvelous new world to Peter; its vigorous, rowdy men, free of narrow traditionalism, opened his mind to a vast store of new ideas and knowledge.*

To escape Sophia's hate, Peter and his mother soon moved from the Kremlin to the village of Preobrazhensk. His only teacher was a scribe of the boyar Duma, one Nikita Zotov, a famous drunkard who was to become one of the young czar's closest friends. Peter, at the age of 10, was virtually illiterate: all he could write properly was his name.

Preobrazhensk bordered on the foreigners' settlement, and there Peter found sanctuary from the odious formality of the court. German comedians came to put on shows in the palace at Preobrazhensk; Peter could go riding, run wild generally, and play at his favorite games. Stable boys, footmen and falconers were the "soldiers" with whom he played, organizing them into military detachments; his companions also included some boys of good family.

On a small tributary of the Moscow River a miniature fortress was built for his pleasure, and little by little his play turned into real war games. He eventually organized some 400 soldiers into "regiments"—modestly, he was satisfied to play the little drummer boy. Peter's war games ought to have warned Sophia that her enemy was growing up; but she was caught up in her own schemes and dreams of becoming Empress.

When Peter reached the age of 17 his mother found a bride for him. An obedient son, he married Eudoxia Lopukhina, a lovely, meek, sensible girl whom he did not love and in whom he showed no interest at all. He was already enthralled by a foreigner, Anna Ivanova Mons, a merchant's daughter whose favors he long enjoyed. He was also wrapped up in his new friends from the *sloboda*: Timmermann, who taught him arithmetic, geography, cosmography and military engineering; and Brandt, who instructed him in naval engineering. On February 19, 1690, Eudoxia gave birth to a son, Alexis, who was fated to play a deeply tragic role in Peter's life.

PETER'S MOCK COURT

Bottom: Peter I during the siege of Azov, in 1696, and, opposite page: the ship Predestination, *built at Voronez between 1698 and 1700 for the fleet in the Sea of Azov. In the first print, the czar, surrounded by a group of aides, including Lefort, Gordon and Golovin, is studying a plan of the fortress, as Timmermann explains it. The war against the Turks, for which the fleet was built, was Czar Peter's first great military undertaking—the first proof that he had learned his lessons in Preobrazhensk well.*

Peter was a giant, nearly seven feet tall, with a powerful physique. He suffered throughout his life, however, from periodic spastic attacks preceded by a wrenching of his neck and violent facial twitching. Zacchary Hults, his personal physician, treated him with a sort of paste made of ground magpies' breasts and wings. Because of these attacks, Peter always slept with a servant at his bedside. In 1684, Peter came down with smallpox, but it had no lasting effects. As a young man, he led a wildly dissolute life, drinking prodigiously, roistering the night through, and gathering around him a band of kindred spirits who were the scandal of all Moscow. By temperament, he found all formality unbearable, all discipline intolerable. But he knew precisely what he wanted and how to get it. Capable of making the sternest sacrifices, he laid down iron-clad rules for himself and his associates.

He organized a parody of the monarchy and clergy, naming as czar a drunkard named Romodanovsky, with a court, throne and chancery, to whom all had to pay homage; as patriarch he named his old tutor Zotov, another notorious drunkard, outfitting him in holy garb, investing him with a miter and cross, and insisting that all respect his "holy" office. His "archbishops" were a group of unregenerate alcoholics; a pig became the symbol of this bacchanalian church. During high feasts, as the real patriarch led the devout through the streets in solemn procession, false archbishops and ecclesiastics would appear, and licentious songs ring out over the sacred hymns; geese, goats and pigs represented the faithful. Peter, however, remained a Christian, though the impulse to mock revered tradition and ingrained custom never left him.

On the opposite page: a Caucasian warrior and a Tatar warrior. Left: reproduction of an original 18th-century watercolor showing a Circassian woman. Below: examples of Caucasian dress. The influence of the East was especially felt in dress. All classes, from the peasants to the merchants and aristocrats, were strongly attached to tradition. In the hodgepodge of countries and regions making up Russia, the deeply rooted differences between the various cultures made deprovincialization of customs extremely difficult; no less arduous was carrying out, if only superficially, the unification of the nation, an aim that Peter pursued with brutal singlemindedness.

19

PLOTS AND COUNTERPLOTS

As Peter proceeded to educate himself, matters at court were gradually getting out of hand. Sophia, the regent, was ambitious and intelligent, but also lazy and easily distracted; her favorite, Prince Golitsyn, was Russia's real ruler. The prince, every inch an aristocrat, was a great admirer of Louis XIV. He lived in a palatial residence sumptuously furnished in the Western style, with a fine library and numerous valuable paintings. A poor general, as his two Crimean campaigns proved, he was nonetheless an astute diplomat, acting with skill in both domestic and foreign affairs. He helped Sophia to combat the intrigues of her enemies, vastly improved the economic and financial situation of the country, and concluded a lasting peace with Poland.

With mounting apprehension, Sophia watched Peter and Ivan grow into young manhood. As regent, her power depended almost entirely on the presence of the *strieltsy*, which had become a sort of Praetorian Guard. In order to ensure their support she even deceived Golitsyn, to take up with their young commander.

When, in desperation, Sophia drew up war plans and mobilized the troops, Peter began gathering supporters about him. A confusing succession of plots and betrayals ensued, but the hand of the czar was growing stronger. Finally, Sophia tried to come to terms with Peter, appealing to the good offices of the patriarch, but the patriarch went over to the czar's side. The *strieltsy*, for the most part, did likewise, actually delivering up their commander for torture and execution. Sophia soon found herself fighting alone. Golitsyn was exiled to Kargopol, on the Arctic Ocean, to get along on the token allowance of a ruble a day for himself and his wife. When Peter returned to Moscow in 1689, Sophia fled to the Convent of Novodevich, where she took the veil.

Opposite page: the
ex-regent Sophia in the convent.
Sophia was ugly and very
fat, with a broad, hairy
face and ulcerated legs.
Above: a wedding
procession in Moscow.
Left: the Monastery of
the Holy Trinity
and, beside it: Eudoxia,
Peter's first wife. The young
Peter was more interested
in a foreigner, Anna Mons;
formerly the mistress of Lefort
and Menshikov, she was
regularly unfaithful to Peter.

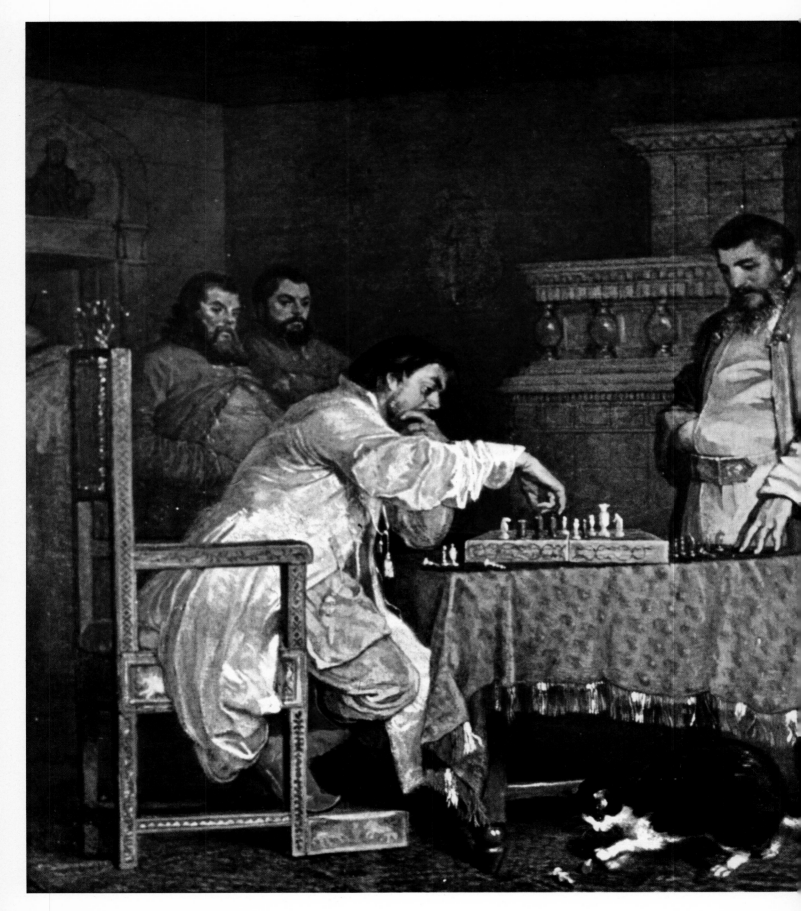

LIVING ON
A GRAND SCALE

Peter's triumph over the regent Sophia caused no outward change in his way of life. The czar had the same taste for street life and street friends that had characterized his adolescence. He continued to find the atmosphere of the Kremlin stuffy beyond endurance, and his wife, who was jealous and forever whining, unbearably oppressive. He ordered his personal residence, with a well-stocked wine cellar, to be built five versts from Preobrazhensk, where his troops were quartered. He also decreed that a house be built in the *sloboda*, where he could give huge parties, because the house of his friend Lefort was too small. The house in the *sloboda* was built of wood to save time, and was large enough to accommodate some 15,000 people. Peter had now decided to do things on a grand scale. When traveling, he insisted on a retinue of at least 300 boyars; in the garden of his personal residence he had wild animals, fountains, pools, and cannon; and waiting at the gates were luxurious carriages drawn by the finest horses to be had.

Left: the czar playing chess.
Right, above: Patrick Gordon,
and, below: François Lefort.
The Scotsman Gordon, who went
to Russia in 1661, served in the
military administration. He was
a man of courage and cultivation,
endowed with high moral
principles. Lefort, born in
Geneva in 1656, was also in the
military. Sharp-witted, lively
and well-balanced, Lefort
shunned intrigue and managed
to remain a close friend of
Peter's. Gordon and Lefort
both exerted considerable
influence on the czar.

RUSSIA'S FIRST FLEET

All his life Peter was plagued by the problem of Russia's inaccessibility to the sea. It was from two Dutchmen he met in the sloboda, Franz Timmermann and Karsten Brandt, that he first heard of Holland and its great sailing ships. Fired with enthusiasm, he persuaded his mother to let him bring an old, English-built boat from Ismailov to the Lake of Pereiaslav, where it was reconditioned. A shipyard was set up at Pereiaslav, with Brandt as director and Peter himself working as a lowly shipfitter. Opposite page: Peter with the old boat. Below: a typical Russian village and a shipyard. Bottom: the first Russian fleet at Archangel.

Peter first saw the sea at the White Sea port of Archangel, and it was there that he determined to build a fleet. But first he had to learn a hard lesson. From July 8 to September 22, 1695, he vainly besieged the Turkish fortress of Azov, on the Black Sea. Withdrawing with heavy casualties, Peter realized that in order to take Azov he needed a real fleet. Returning to Moscow on November 22, he immediately started drawing up plans. Shipyards were set up at Voronez, on the River Don. Peter had whole forests felled and shipwrights from all over Europe brought in. It was an imposing naval squadron that weighed anchor on May 3, 1696, with the czar himself on the galley *Principium* as Captain Peter Alexevich. Thanks to the ships built at Voronez, Azov's fate was sealed: overland, an army led by the boyar Schein closed in on the fortress; from the sea it was attacked by an assortment of large and small galleys, fire ships, barks and lighters, and was eventually forced to capitulate. This marked Peter's first military success and transformed the impetuous, headstrong youth into a grown man. Meanwhile, the only person Peter had ever truly loved, his mother Natalia, died—and with her Eudoxia's sole protectress. Peter began to turn over in his mind ways to be rid of his wife once and for all.

OLD RUSSIA SCANDALIZED: PETER'S JOURNEY ABROAD

Peter's subjects never had to wait long for royal scandal. The first genuinely serious occasion arose when the czar decided to go abroad. He first announced his intention to the Duma, then proceeded to organize an enormous caravan (2,000,000 rubles in cash, furs, precious silks, and other items). He would travel "incognito" as plain Peter Mikhailov. He appointed the Swiss Lefort his chief of mission, and assembled a retinue of noblemen and scribes, a court steward, a majordomo, four chamberlains, four dwarfs, a jester, physicians, surgeons, trumpeters, a wine waiter, a quartermaster, a chef, lackeys, serfs, servants, coachmen, and 70 soldiers. The caravan itself totaled 32 carriages, four wagons, and 34 horses.

Holland and England were the main countries visited. Everywhere the Russians were greeted with honor and curiosity, even though their behavior—notably Peter's—gave rise to more than a few incidents. He left no doubt wherever he went that he was not cut out for the pomp of royal courts and noble houses: a slovenly, bullying giant of a man who could barely manipulate a knife and fork, who caroused with workers and sailors and who consumed prodigious quantities of food and wine. But Peter had not intended to frequent polite society anyway. Uncultivated, thirsting for knowledge, he went into mills and shipyards, artisans' shops and museums, hospitals and almshouses. Architecture, mechanics, printing, shipbuilding, medicine, surgery, dentistry, anatomy, and design—all interested him tremendously. For him, an idea had value only insofar as it could be put to use: no sooner had he learned something than he wanted to try it out. In Amsterdam he had himself taken on in the shipyard of the East India Company, where a frigate was built especially for him so that he could follow the various phases of the work. As soon as he had acquired a little knowledge of dentistry, he used his subjects as guinea pigs, yanking teeth indiscriminately. When he realized that there were many who could not stomach watching an anatomy lesson, he made his associates cut the tendons of a cadaver with their teeth.

The legend of Peter's stay in Saardam, an important Dutch shipbuilding center, has been much embroidered. Actually, the czar stayed there only eight days, quartered in the simple smith's dwelling shown to the left. To the right, above and bottom: two more scenes from the stay in Saardam; in the middle: Königsberg, Peter's first important stop. There the czar met the Elector of Brandenburg and the Princess Sophia-Charlotte, a woman of great intelligence and refinement, a friend and correspondent of Leibnitz. In the center: an oil painting by Abraham Storck showing Peter, visible in the skiff, visiting ships in Amsterdam harbor.

A BURNING THIRST FOR KNOWLEDGE

Peter's visit to England was largely prompted by what he had heard about the high level of English shipbuilding. England at that time rivaled Holland in this field. The czar was picked up in Holland by the royal yacht, commanded by Admiral Mitchell, and reached London two days later. He was assigned a most congenial guide, the eccentric Earl of Caermarthen, a mighty drinker, to whom Peter took an immediate liking. Left and right, above: two views of the royal docks at Deptford. Lower left: the czar visiting the Deptford shipyard. Lower right: the docks at Woolwich.

Leaving his retinue behind in Holland, Peter went on to London, where he continued to display a consuming curiosity about things and an unquenchable thirst for knowledge. His easygoing but rough ways aroused first the perplexity and eventually the annoyance of the English. He was lodged in a splendid house, once the home of the widow of Charles II; the czar immediately transformed it into a mews. There was such a stable stench that when the king came to call he asked that the window be opened, despite the cold.

Peter was an efficient tourist: he carefully visited everything he felt it important to see. As usual, the things that struck him were not monuments or great works of art, but rather the work of craftsmen, and technical and scientific achievements. He was fascinated by the Greenwich Observatory; he had a watchmaker show him how to disassemble and reassemble clocks; he was delighted by the perfection achieved by English coffin makers; he visited the Deptford shipyard and the cannon foundry at Woolwich; he went to Oxford, where the honorary degree of doctor of laws was conferred on him. On the lighter side, he took a fancy to the actress Mary Cross and attended several plays; he sailed on the Thames; and he swilled liquor with sailors and workers as if there were no tomorrow. For his pleasure, a mock naval battle was held near the Isle of Wight. When he departed, the English breathed a sigh of relief.

Peter left England on May 9, returning to Amsterdam, then on to Vienna, where he planned to discuss with the Emperor Leopold the question of prosecuting the war against the Turks. Leopold received the Russian czar, but nothing concrete came from their talks. Peter was strangely intimidated by the emperor and the court atmosphere and, eager to move on to Venice, left further negotiations to his diplomats. In any case, he had already derived all possible benefit from his journey: he had not only learned a great deal but had also drawn Europe's attention to his person and country.

Below, left: William and Mary of England. Right: Greenwich Observatory. Bottom: a portrait of Peter painted by Godfrey Kneller during the czar's stay in London, and the fireplace surmounted by Robert Norden's compass chart and star map in the Royal Gallery

in Kensington Palace. Peter was more interested in the compass chart than in the palace's great collections. Opposite page, above: Kensington Palace. Below: the London Mint, which Peter visited, taking a great interest in advanced methods of minting.

A HASTY RETURN HOME

Peter did not get to Venice. In Vienna, word reached him that the *strieltsy* had rebelled and were marching on the capital. In Cracow, as he hurried toward home, he learned that the boyar Schein had defeated the rebels; this news gave him enough time there to meet with Augustus II of Saxony, the new King of Poland. The two monarchs drew up plans for a war against Sweden. Peter had not forgotten that Russia needed an outlet to the sea, and that sea had to be the Baltic.

Peter returned to Moscow with one thought uppermost in his mind—to punish the *strieltsy*. The czar's grand tour ended in a blood bath, as, for that matter, it had begun: before setting out, he had uncovered a plot in which Sophia was involved, quelling it by a wholesale slaughter of the culprits. This time, the rebellion seemed much more widespread. The punitive fury Peter unleashed against the *strieltsy* was partly an effort to draw attention away from the deep underlying reasons for the revolt—general discontent and, among conservative elements of the country, resistance to change.

MASSACRE OF THE STRIELTSY

In 14 torture chambers, the torturers, assisted by Peter and his friends, worked to extract from the *strieltsy* confessions and proof of their guilt. The horrors lasted for days, from morning till night.

Peter blamed his half-sister Sophia for the revolt. She had indeed had a hand in it; but the uprising had more serious causes. Discontent was strongest in the *strieltsy*, which had long controlled the country and its rulers unopposed. Accustomed to almost unlimited power and privileges, they resented being stationed far from their families in Moscow and sent to rot in barracks on the distant borders of Lithuania and Azov, with the unhappy prospect of seeing their corps demobilized and replaced by regular regiments organized along European lines. Moreover, Peter's absence from Moscow made it possible for feelings of discontent and opposition to grow in other quarters. There were Old Ritualists ever ready to identify Peter with Antichrist; there were priests and boyars whom Peter had treated with disrespect and who were uncompromisingly against his reforms; and there was the populace at large, unwilling to break with tradition and the faith of their fathers.

After quelling the revolt, Schein had punished the *strieltsy*, putting a number of them to death, together with their leaders. But Peter was not satisfied with mere punishment. He demanded slaughter, a massacre that would strike such terror in the hearts of his adversaries and of Russians everywhere that further rebellion or even protest would be unthinkable. A trial was held, and a tremendous blood bath followed. A thousand *strieltsy* were sentenced to die, some by hanging, others by beheading. Peter was particularly furious because, despite the cruel imaginativeness he dis-

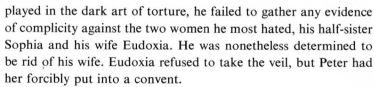

Left: a dramatic painting of Peter's repression of the strieltsy *revolt, with Peter on horseback waiting for the condemned men to be brought forward. Some displayed uncommon courage, notably one, known as "Eagle," who swept the head of the man who had preceded him from the execution block and said, "I'll put my own here now." Peter pardoned him. In two engravings of the period: loyalist troops combating the* strieltsy (*above*), *and the execution of the rebels* (*below*).

played in the dark art of torture, he failed to gather any evidence of complicity against the two women he most hated, his half-sister Sophia and his wife Eudoxia. He was nonetheless determined to be rid of his wife. Eudoxia refused to take the veil, but Peter had her forcibly put into a convent.

Freed of his marital cares, he turned with fresh vigor to the torture of the *strieltsy*. Despite the intercession of the patriarch Adrian, the condemned soldiers were carried into Red Square in wagons, where they were variously hanged, beheaded, impaled and buried alive. The czar himself beheaded some of the condemned men and forced his courtiers to do likewise. Only Lefort and Colonel Blomberg refused; many reportedly were amused and actually enjoyed themselves. For months the bodies went unburied. Some of the corpses swung outside Sophia's cell window. Others were hung on hooks near the Kremlin gates.

At the height of the massacre, Peter took time to carouse with his "maddest, most mock and drunken Synod," a band of rowdy friends who engaged in tremendous drinking bouts, sacrilegious processions, huge banquets, orgies and riotous invasions of private homes.

SHORN BEARDS AND SHORTENED CLOTHES

Left: a Russian drawing dating from the early 18th century, showing a "reactionary's" beard being cut off. Below: Peter in a Polish caftan (left), and dressed as a sailor. Bottom: a textile shop (left), and a caftan being shortened, following Peter's decrees. The clergy constituted Peter's main opposition, and the czar did not forget it.

In 1721, helped by Bishop Feofan Prokopovich, the church was "beheaded"—deprived of its patriarch. The patriarchy was replaced by a Holy Governing Synod presided over by the czar himself; this was done, it was explained, "lest the spiritual authority be considered better and higher than the temporal authority."

Many of the Petrine reforms, as Peter's more beneficial acts were called, took their toll in blood and injustice. The actions of a ruler of such a backward, semi-barbaric country as the Russia of the 17th and 18th centuries cannot be judged according to contemporary morality and sensitivity. And yet, Peter's utter bestiality and the icy cruelty of his first acts as czar seem an unnecessarily harsh way to transform Russia into a modern, Western country.

Peter returned from Europe ready to introduce at least one Western innovation: he promptly "reformed" the Russian beard, starting by personally shaving off those of General Schein and Romodanovsky, ranking members of his inner circle; he then went after the beards of all the boyars he could lay hands on. This was an offense not only to male vanity but to the Russian faith. A Russian's beard was obvious material proof that he had been created "in the image of God." Without his beard, he became an animal. But Peter had noticed that beards were a rarity in the West, and so he decreed that everyone except country folk was to shave. Beards were strictly outlawed. Only later was the law modified: a man might have a beard provided he paid a heavy tax and wore a medal with the inscription, "Beards are a ridiculous ornament."

Having taken Draconian measures with regard to superfluous hair, Peter turned his attention to clothing. Two decrees, in 1700 and 1701, imposed short Western-style clothes on the entire populace, with only the clergy and peasantry excluded. Not all of Peter's reforms were so arbitrary or, in retrospect, so amusing. Courtiers were obliged to participate in court life, with women attending receptions and playing an active role in society. The Julian calendar was adopted and the Cyrillic alphabet was simplified. Peter succeeded in overcoming all resistance to his reforms, but at the price of establishing a police state. Eventually, the police intruded everywhere, checking to see that the citizens were shaved, dressed, and occupied in prescribed ways; that they did not spend too much; and that they raised their children on sound principles.

FOUNDING THE RUSSIAN ACADEMY

Peter was extremely aware of the importance of education. He returned from England with a Mr. Ferguson, a naval expert, and in 1701 founded a School of Mathematical and Naval Sciences. Unfortunately, the students who were enrolled were nearly all illiterate. Peter sought to remedy this situation by setting up a number of schools. The first Russian newspaper, *Vedomosti* (*News*), which began publication on January 2, 1703, indicates that in 1703 mathematics students in Moscow numbered 300 and philosophy students 45. Peter's educational reforms were far from systematic. He founded an Academy of Sciences when there was still an acute shortage of elementary schools; he imported from Germany 17 professors who, lacking students, had to listen to one another's lectures. Peter also saw to it that a number of books were translated into Russian. His choices were in keeping with his utilitarian concept of culture—dictionaries, treatises on arithmetic, geometry, military engineering, even a book of etiquette.

Opposite page, above: two woodcuts of the period showing a printing shop and a paper mill. Center: a Tatar school in the Crimea. Bottom: a bookshop in Peter's time. On this page: a school in Muscovy. In the Russia of Peter's day, schools existed but were poorly attended. Lack of equipment and effective teaching methods made them virtually useless. There were neither teachers nor textbooks, and the disciplinary measures taken by teachers were incredibly severe. Thus illiteracy continued widespread, even among the nobility and clergy. Reading was all but unheard of, and an utter rarity was the man who spoke a foreign language. Interesting and perhaps indicative of the attitude toward foreign languages is the Russian word nemez (German), from the same root as "to become mute," as if whoever did not speak Russian might as well have been mute.

On this page: Charles XII of Sweden in a portrait of the French School, and (below) Charles II at the Battle of Narva (top of a tankard, 1701). The Battle of Narva is also the subject of the engraving by Romejn de Hooghe on the opposite page, above. Peter deluded himself into thinking that he could take Narva as easily as he had taken Azov, which made his defeat all the more stinging. After Narva he announced he was willing to sue for peace. He asked Holland and the King of England to act as mediators, clumsily trying to cloak his fear in "pacifism."

CHARLES XII: LION OF THE NORTH

On this page, bottom: Ivan Mazepa recounting his life to Charles XII. Mazepa became hetman (chief, or headman) of the Ukrainian Cossacks in 1687. During his first campaigns against the Turks he supported the czar, who trusted him blindly. Little by little, Mazepa moved toward the camp of Charles XII. He remains a rather enigmatic figure in Russian history: according to some, he was driven by personal ambition; others feel he was struggling for Ukrainian independence. In either case, the Ukraine profited greatly from his rule.

The meeting between Peter and Augustus II, King of Poland, led to the Treaty of Preobrazhensk on November 11, 1699. Poland, Denmark and Russia were united against Sweden which, under the leadership of the child prodigy King Charles XII, was the strongest of the Northern powers. It was disastrous for Peter that, in his efforts to find an outlet to the sea for Russia, he should have had to confront Sweden. He no doubt underestimated his adversary. Though barely 18, Charles XII possessed unusual qualities as a warrior. He lived a Spartan life, paying no attention to dress, eating little and hurriedly, drinking only beer and sleeping without sheets or blankets. The only precious object he owned was a gilt Bible, which he was often seen reading. Declaring that he was wed to his army, he remained scrupulously chaste. Intrigue and the subtleties of diplomacy were alien to him, and he made decisions quickly, without asking advice. He was not without learning, indeed often conversed in Latin, and read for pleasure. He enjoyed war for its own sake, with no thirst for conquest (when offered the crown of Poland, he refused it). He proved his genius as a military strategist, dealing the Russians a humiliating defeat when they laid seige to the port of Narva with forces three times the strength of his own. Peter personally made a very poor showing in the battle. Seeing that the tide was running against him, he quickly turned his army over to Prince Charles of Croy, who had been dispatched by Poland to get news of operations; then, disguised as a peasant, he ran away, abandoning spoils that included nearly 150 cannon, numerous mortars and other military equipment, provisions, flags, the war chest, and several generals among the prisoners, not to mention 10,000 dead on the field. If Charles had taken full advantage of his victory and marched on Moscow, nothing would have stood in his way. Instead he turned on Augustus, dealing him a series of stunning blows. Gaining control of all of Poland, he installed a new sovereign, Stanislas Leczynski, on the throne.

Below: two commemorative medals struck on the fall of Narva in 1704, and of Nöteborg in 1702. Right: portrait of Menshikov, and lower right: a regimental standard during the reign of Peter the Great. Alexander D. Menshikov, born in 1673, rose under Peter's protection from pastry cook's helper to the highest honors of the imperial régime: he held the rank of general and the title of prince. His star did not wane even after the czar's death. A favorite of the widowed empress, Catherine I, whose accession he had supported, he ruled Russia in her place until, falling into disgrace in 1727, he was exiled to Siberia, where he died two years later.

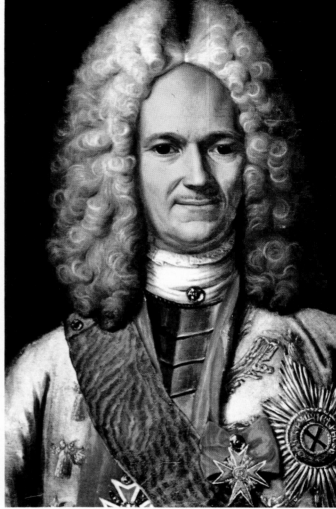

THE CZAR DOES NOT GIVE UP

Below: Menshikov being crowned with the laurel, an allegorical print dating from 1714. This Russian engraving, crowded with symbols and inscriptions exalting the valor and glory of the prince, commemorates one of the highest points in the career of a man whom the poet Pushkin called "an almost sovereign potentate."

Equally brilliant in war and statecraft, fluent in several foreign languages, Alexander D. Menshikov made himself indispensable to the czar. He was also a shameless thief and profiteer, as was proved by an inquiry that Peter ordered in 1711. Menshikov was nonetheless allowed to continue to hold positions of responsibility.

Charles XII's failure to pursue total victory gave Peter time to catch his breath, and he abandoned the idea of suing for peace. Although he realized he was in a difficult position, he was not the sort of man to give up. He had been dealt a crippling blow, but was able to turn it to good use. From personal experience he now understood the military inadequacies of his country, the total disorganization of the army. Russia's prestige abroad had suffered a severe setback, and discontent, always latent at home, was seething just beneath the surface. Peter's answer to this was, typically, to institute a number of reforms: compulsory conscription; the requisitioning of church and monastery bells to make cannon; and the forced mobilization of the general populace, including women and priests, for the building of border fortifications. Once his forces had been reconstituted and strengthened, hostilities were resumed. While Charles was bogged down in what Peter called "the Polish quagmire," little by little, in 1701 and 1702, the Russians occupied Livonia and Estonia. Peter himself participated in one operation, the taking of the fortress of Nöteborg. The city was defended by only 100 soldiers, who put up a valiant fight. Following its seizure, Nöteborg was renamed Schlüsselburg ("key city," as it was the key to Finland), and Alexander D. Menshikov was appointed governor. All the officers who took part in the campaign against Sweden shared in the triumph, which was celebrated in Moscow with a huge, spectacular ceremony.

During the war Peter also found time to concern himself with a Russian fleet. Fearful that the Turks would take advantage of his difficulties, he raced ahead with the construction of ships at Voronez. The Russian navy eventually became a formidable instrument of war, proving itself in victorious encounters with the Swedes on Lake Peipus and Lake Ladoga.

THE FOUNDING OF ST. PETERSBURG

St. Petersburg came into being at a difficult moment in Peter I's career. For years, the war with Sweden had dragged on, with the Russians suffering defeat after defeat. The state treasury was almost depleted, and Peter was forced to devise new schemes for squeezing money from his subjects. He appropriated tax monies paid to market owners; the state took over the postal monopoly and the administration of hotels and hostels; public bathhouses were subjected to taxation, as were salt and tobacco and even coffins. The ruble was further devalued and, while this helped the financial situation at home, it weakened Russia's economic position abroad, where enormous debts were accumulating. There were troubles in Peter's private life as well: in the pocket of the Saxon envoy Kienigseck, who died of drowning, he found a note proving that his mistress, Anna Mons, had betrayed him. He had her arrested, together with 30 presumed accomplices. Anna escaped execution, and even lived to marry the Prussian ambassador.

The czar's life was still punctuated by orgies and outbursts of sheer bestiality: some nuns were put to death owing to a misunderstanding; alleged visitors to his repudiated wife Eudoxia were impaled; and once again some of the *strieltsy* were tortured and executed, following a revolt on the Don. Progressive acts went hand in hand with these and other outrages: a huge almshouse was constructed; the Cyrillic alphabet was simplified; a military hospital and a surgical hospital were established; the army was strengthened; the first efficient arms and munitions factories went into production; and ever increasing attention was paid to the navy. It was with a Baltic navy in mind that the new city of St. Petersburg was founded. Formerly a tiny Finnish fishing village and, centuries earlier, the fortified depot of Novgorod, it was situated in a bleak landscape of forests and vast frozen swamps. Few except Peter saw any practical value in the site.

Center: Peter I at the founding of St. Petersburg in 1703.
Below: two 18th-century engravings, showing Peter visiting the shipyard during construction of the city, and Admiralty Square. The building of the new capital took a heavy toll in human life.

As early as 1696, after the conquest of Azov, Peter planned to build a new capital in Ingria, at the mouth of the Neva. His journey to Holland and England spurred his plans: he wanted a port—a gateway to the West—that would serve his expansionist policies.

Below: Peter I during the construction of St. Petersburg. Opposite page, above and bottom: two views of the city in the time of Peter I, showing the Neva and a bridge over the river. Center: Peter's model house in present-day Leningrad. The building of St. Petersburg went ahead with breathtaking rapidity, especially considering the difficulties that had to be overcome. Skilled and unskilled workers, for the most part pressed into labor battalions, had to travel many miles for stone, earth and other building materials. There was a lack of the most fundamental tools and instruments, not to mention deplorable housing facilities and insufficient food. It was some years later that families of quality came to consider it a social necessity to move from Moscow to Peter's city on the Neva.

A CITY BUILT BY FORCE OF WILL

As usual, Peter had to overcome widespread resistance, incomprehension and hostility. His methods were direct. He began by having a wooden house built for himself on one of the isles in the Neva; he then insisted that his associates and favorites do likewise. Was stone needed for building purposes? Very well: he forbade the use of stone in the rest of the country. The work force too small? Forced labor, then. Legend has perhaps exaggerated the number of deaths due to the construction of St. Petersburg, but it was high—very high. The general population was drawn upon for common labor, though foremen, master builders, engineers and architects were imported. These technicians were mostly German, Dutch, English and Italian. In 1703, for instance, an Italian architect, Domenico Trezzini, arrived from Denmark. Having long worked in Northern Europe, he was eminently suited for handling northern architectural styles, and held the post of chief architect even after the arrival of the Frenchman Leblond, who drew up the first city plan, and the Germans Schluter and Schadel. Foreign technicians worked together, often on the same building, which made for a blend of architectural styles. St. Petersburg is a superb example of a city planned in its smallest details: Peter not only compelled every high dignitary to build a house, but to build it in a particular way. Each, according to his rank or occupation, was assigned a building site; the dimensions, plan, and building materials were all rigidly fixed by the czar's architects. The obligation to build a house, in brick or stone, of one or two stories, was incumbent on every citizen, depending on his means. Situated in the heart of one of the most charming river areas in Europe, the city proved of strategic and commercial value. And it was the outlet to the sea that Peter had sought.

A GRIM
FAMILY DRAMA

Peter had only one child, Alexis, by his wife Eudoxia. The trial and death of his son tragically colored the final years of Peter's reign. Despite all efforts made to justify Peter's actions, in the light of reasons of state, his responsibility remains, and remains serious. Peter unleashed against his son all the cruelty of which he was capable. It is difficult to imagine two more different personalities and temperaments. Peter was impetuous, violent, self-willed; Alexis was a weakling, hesitant, impressionable. Alexis' character was not strengthened by the upbringing he received: he was utterly neglected from the day the convent door closed behind his repudiated mother. Thanks to Eudoxia, Alexis grew up religious, superstitious and reactionary. The one trait he had in common with his father was a taste for liquor. An alcoholic from early youth, he had no interest in politics or the military life. He feared his father, until he learned to hate him instead. He was fairly intelligent; he

knew some mathematics, drew well, and spoke and wrote German. But the strongest influence on him was the clergy, particularly a certain Ignatiev, who was violently opposed to the Petrine reforms.

After Peter's second marriage, he tried to win his son's loyalty through generosity. He offered journeys, a wife, and administrative and military responsibilities. All to no avail; and gradually Peter came to detest him. But he was also afraid of him, for Alexis could well become a rallying point for the discontented and reactionary forces in the nation.

His tongue loosened by alcohol, Alexis made harsh criticisms of his father; when he was drunk, he made no secret of his intention to suppress all the Petrine reforms as soon as his father died. Informers brought Peter word of his son's plans—the destruction of his entire lifework. Alexis' fate was sealed.

Left: Princesses Anna and Elizabeth, daughters of Peter and Catherine. Elizabeth, who became empress in 1741, died in 1762. Below: Alexis in an 18th-century engraving. Right: portrait of Princess Sophia-Charlotte of Brunswick-Wölfenbüttel, wife of Alexis.

The marriage between Alexis and the German princess, arranged by Peter, took place in 1711. Though his wife was kind and gentle, Alexis, influenced by the more reactionary members of the clergy, not only loathed her but suspected her of heresy because she was a Lutheran. The poor princess was homely and flat-chested, with a face pitted with smallpox scars. Alexis mistreated her unmercifully. She died in childbirth in 1715. While she was still alive, Alexis took a mistress, a vulgar Finnish serving girl and prostitute, who later testified against him, helping to bring about his downfall.

THE UNDOING OF CHARLES XII

Left: Peter I in a portrait dated 1718. Directly below, and bottom: two scenes from the Battle of Poltava. Center: the capture of Swedish ships in May, 1703. The long war against Sweden demanded enormous sacrifices of Russia. More than once Peter found himself on the brink of total ruin. His greatest opponent was young King Charles XII. The great final victory at Poltava signaled the twilight of Swedish might and the rise of Russian power under Czar Peter I.

As St. Petersburg grew, the war against Sweden continued in seesaw fashion. Charles XII imposed a new king on Poland, and the Russian army advanced toward Kurland and Riga. In the crucial Battle of Gemavers, the Russians were soundly defeated, although they managed to take Mittau, the capital of Kurland. Charles XII then decided to play for higher stakes, by carrying the war into the heart of enemy territory. In December, 1707, the Swedes laid seige to Grodno and took it. This created an extremely serious situation for the Russians: the capture of Grodno gave Charles an open road to Moscow and imperiled all of Peter's conquests along the Baltic. The two Russian commanders beat an inglorious retreat, providentially helped by ice on the River Nieman which held up the Swedes: if it had not, the entire Russian army would have fallen into Charles' hands. The czar, remaining at St. Petersburg to protect the Baltic regions, left the defense of Moscow in Menshikov's hands. Bogged down for a time in Lithuania by uninterrupted rains, Charles XII eventually reached the little Beresina River, where he defeated a Russian detachment and crossed over, then pushed on to the Bibitsch. When flooded, this river seemed almost impassable; across it lay a swamp and, farther off, the Russians had entrenched themselves behind a parapet mounted with cannon. Undaunted, Charles and his troops plunged into the river under Russian fire, managing to make their way through the swamp. After seven consecutive charges, the Russians fell back. Charles pushed onward, but was halted by the Russians at Mogilev. Further Swedish reverses followed at Dobroe and Lesnoe. Charles eventually found himself faced with the decision of driving east, toward Moscow, or south, toward the Ukraine. His mistake was to take the latter course.

*Above: Zaporogian Cossacks.
Right: an engraving of
the Battle of Lesnoe
(September 28, 1708). Beside
it: two Cossack soldiers
in front of the Kremlin.
Far right: an 18th-century
print of a Cossack. The
Zaporogian Cossacks were a
semi-barbaric people. The word
Cossack (qazaq in Turkish-
Tatar, meaning vagabond) tells
something of their character; the
"Zaporogians" were Cossacks
za porogi (from "below the
rapids" of the Dnieper).*

THE COSSACKS SWITCH SIDES

Charles XII committed a serious error when he hoped to get help from the Ukrainian Cossacks, and in particular from their chief, or *hetman*, Ivan Mazepa. A man of 70 at the time, Mazepa could boast long and faithful years of service to Peter. The czar had always been generous to him, refusing to believe any unfavorable reports concerning the *hetman*. Yet the wily Mazepa had long been in contact with Charles XII. From the *hetman* Charles expected to receive provisions, which the Swedish forces badly needed, as well as ammunition, artillery and a large contingent of soldiers. Mazepa, who encouraged wild hopes of Ukrainian independence among the Cossacks, was able to play on their discontent; their traditionalist feelings had been wounded by Peter's reforms. And even the non-Cossack Ukrainians were untrustworthy: on the one hand, the people did not mind seeing the Russians replace the Poles; on the other, the nobility found the domination of either intolerable. Commitments and promises were virtually worthless in such a climate. The *hetman* long managed to steer a course clear of difficulties—until he found himself trapped in the web of his own duplicity. When Charles was defeated at Lesnoe, Mazepa realized that the tide was turning in favor of Peter. Now he was eager to switch sides. His Cossacks, however, were already moving to Charles' assistance. On October 31, 1708, the Russians took Baturino, and Mazepa was utterly deserted by his people: a new *hetman* was elected in his place, and the clergy declared itself loyal to Peter. Mazepa was hanged in effigy and some of his collaborators were broken on the wheel. Even without the Cossacks' help (negligible as it turned out to be) Charles remained a formidable enemy. But his army was at the end of its tether: cold, hunger and disease had decimated the Swedish main force. It straggled through Russian villages and found that the villagers had left, burning everything behind them. Charles' scant knowledge of the terrain made his situation even more difficult; and Peter cleverly let him wear himself out, biding his time.

A DECISIVE VICTORY

The Battle of Poltava marked a turning point for the Swedes. First, the city was stocked with provisions; second, it lay across one of the main routes to Moscow. Charles laid siege to it in early March, 1709. Throughout the winter Peter had played a waiting game, partly to exhaust the Swedish forces and partly because he feared a Turkish attack from the rear. Now he assembled his troops and prepared for battle. His army was magnificently outfitted, with an abundance of cannon, provisions and medical supplies. On June 15, some 70,000 Russians arrived under the walls of Poltava. Facing them was a decimated army suffering from every sort of privation. Peter prepared his attack carefully. First he dug a long trench between himself and the enemy and stationed cavalry between two forests, covering them with artillery. He then drew up a plan of attack, designating himself as commander in chief, with a general each in charge of the two flanks and the center: Bauer, Menshikov and Sheremetev. Charles was still suffering from a foot wound when he got word that the Russians were preparing to attack. He decided to seize the initiative. Both sides fought heroically. With seemingly little regard for his life, the czar exposed himself to enemy fire: a bullet pierced his hat and another lodged in his saddle. Charles was carried from the field on a litter. After two hours' fighting the Swedish forces were routed. Charles himself was forced to retreat, clinging, in agonizing pain, to his horse. Ten thousand Swedes were left on the field; 10,000 more were taken prisoner, soon to be pressed into work on St. Petersburg. Peter celebrated the victory with a banquet, to which he invited high dignitaries and officers he had taken prisoner. Raising a goblet, he toasted "the health of His Majesty, the King of Sweden, master of the art of warfare." Naturally exultant, he forgot that it was not the Swedish army he had defeated, but a bare shadow of what had once been a mighty war machine. Still, he was not the only person to be deluded: the rest of Europe, too, thought that Charles had been defeated by the sheer force of Russian arms; this certainly helped to increase Peter's prestige. The czar had only one complaint: his son Alexis, a quartermaster commissar, had not participated in the battle—he had been sick, or at least had so pleaded. The high-water mark in Peter's military career was reached with the Battle of Poltava.

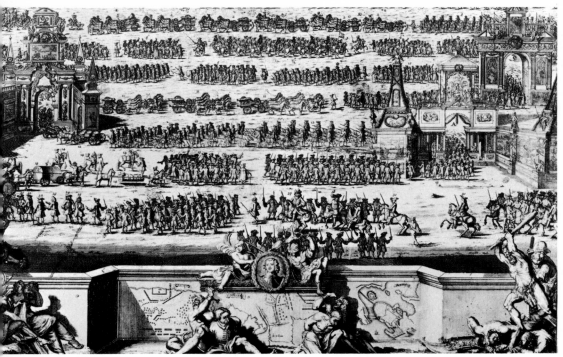

Above: the Battle of Poltava. Left: an engraving showing the triumphant return of Russian troops to Moscow after defeating the Swedish army. The victory at Poltava has been amply treated in Russian and foreign literature. The most famous work on the subject is a poem by Pushkin, published in 1829. Poltava figures in the annals of Russian history for the first time in 1174; it was then called Ltava. Ceded along with Glinsk in the 15th century to the Tatars of Lithuania, it became Russian in 1667, then was an important Cossack fortress and headquarters of the Poltava Regiment.

54

CATHERINE, A WISE ADVISER

Left: a painting that shows, during the reign of Czar Alexis, what was called the "czarina's spring coming-out" to Mass. Below: Czarevich Peter, the son of Peter the Great and Catherine. The child died very young, in 1719.

The victorious Battle of Poltava was celebrated in Moscow with a triumphal feast. Charles XII, who escaped to take refuge with the Turks, was to remain a thorn in Peter's side. He had even held on to his treasury, besides, it seems, the riches of Mazepa, who had committed suicide. For a time, Peter went from victory to victory: he took Vyborg, then Riga.

Meanwhile, the Turks, under a sultan cleverly incited by Charles, were preparing to do battle with the Russians again. In 1710, diplomatic relations between Russia and Turkey were broken off. Immediately afterward, the sultan declared war on the czar. But, before joining his army, Peter attended to a personal matter: he wanted to lend official sanction to his liaison with Catherine, his current mistress. Born Martha Skavronskaia, this Livonian servant girl had been a favorite of Sheremetev and Menshikov before enthralling the czar. She was endowed with considerable intelligence and a strong character. Peter presented her to his relatives, announcing that he intended to marry her as soon as he found time. Meanwhile, Catherine was to be treated as his legal consort, with the title of Highness.

The war, when it began, was disastrous for the czar. Peter and his troops eventually found themselves isolated and cut off from supplies. On one side stood the Turkish vizier with his Janizaries, on another the Tatars, and on yet another the Turkish artillery. There was no chance even of sending for reinforcements. Peter felt all was lost. It was Catherine who wisely suggested opening negotiations. Peter was prepared to make great concessions, to relinquish Azov and the coastline to the sultan and to give Livonia to Sweden; he was also prepared to pay a heavy indemnity. To his great astonishment, the Turkish conditions were mild: Peter had only to give up Azov and the hinterland, to promise not to meddle in Polish affairs, and to permit the unhindered passage home of Charles XII.

Above: Catherine, in an 18th-century engraving, persuading Peter to sign the Treaty of Pruth. Catherine's role in the war between Russia and Turkey was considerable and contributed to raising the czar's morale. Peter remained eternally grateful to her.

MARRIAGE AND PEACE

Charles XII was sorely disappointed on learning of the agreement reached between the Russians and Turks; Peter, on the other hand, was delighted to have got off so lightly. On March 12, 1712, he was officially married to Catherine. The marriage seems to have met, at home and abroad, with general approval.

In the following years, the czar continued to wage war: the Russian army and fleet took Finland. It was then that Peter's military might began to cast a shadow across not only Sweden but all the rest of Europe. Chancelleries and the press, even in countries with treaty obligations against Sweden, began to take a critical, even hostile, attitude toward Russia. Relations between Peter and the Austrian emperor, Charles VI, so deteriorated that Peter felt it necessary to find a powerful ally; this need, among others, took him to France in 1717. The visit, however, yielded little: Peter was able to get no more than vague promises of neutrality from the French. At last, weary of war, worried about the negative effects permanent mobilization was having at home, and wishing to get on with his domestic reforms, Peter decided to conclude a peace treaty with Sweden. This took time because his old opponent, Charles XII, had died in 1718 on a minor campaign against Danish Norway. Desultory hostilities were resumed, but finally, in 1721, after a series of separate agreements, the Peace Treaty of Nystad was signed, ending the Great Northern War after 21 years. Sweden resumed control of most of Finland, and Russia kept Livonia, Karelia, Estonia and Ingria. The Treaty of Nystad was greeted with jubilation by the Russian populace and was celebrated in Moscow with a huge masked ball. The Treaty of Nystad marked the death of old Muscovy and the birth of Russia. The land Peter wrested from Sweden assured Russia of an outlet to the sea and control of the Baltic.

Opposite page: detail of a
royal marriage ceremony (above),
and Peter's marriage to Catherine
(below). On this page, above:
a wedding in a family of boyars.
Left: a portrait of Catherine,
and the interior of a Russian
house. Peter was married wearing
the uniform of a rear admiral.
No ministers or members of the
aristocracy were present at the
ceremony. At the conclusion
of the rites, a huge wedding
breakfast was served, followed
by a ball and fireworks.

A FRUITLESS JOURNEY

Peter set out on his second journey abroad in an entirely different spirit from the first time. The czar was now a powerful sovereign, victor over the Swedes at Poltava and the man who had transformed Russia from a semi-barbaric state into a nation that commanded respect. Above all, he left with a precise aim in mind: he wanted an ally on whom he could count in furthering his expansionist aims against Sweden and Turkey. In Paris a magnificent suite of apartments was reserved for him in the Louvre, but he chose to take up more modest lodgings in the ducal Palais Lesdiguières. Once through with the formalities demanded by a state visit, Peter set about satisfying his thirst for knowledge. He wanted to see all that Paris had to offer; displaying exceptional physical endurance, he pursued daily programs that no normal man could have stood. He visited Versailles, and called on Mme. de Maintenon, Louis XIV's favorite, but by then an invalid. Princes and great men vied with one another to be received by the czar, and Peter saw them all; he visited palaces and monuments, but also poked into side streets and the poorer working-class districts. The two things that most impressed him were the manufacture of Gobelin tapestries and the Mint. At the Mint he discovered, to his surprise, that a medal bearing his likeness was being minted. Peter was awestruck: unknown to him, the famous artist Jean Duvivier had seen him and had so clearly fixed his features in his memory that he had been able to reproduce them.

Peter's major aim in visiting France was not fulfilled: he proposed, quite bluntly, that a diplomatic and military alliance between France and Russia be established; he wanted to replace Sweden in the scheme of European power blocs. But this would have upset France's system of alliances in eastern Europe.

Left: Peter's travel chest, with compartments for bottles. Below: Peter I meeting the young Louis XV at the Palais Lesdiguières. On this occasion Peter scandalized the courtiers by taking the boy king up in his arms. Actually, Peter gave his hosts many reasons to be scandalized, as he had during his first trip abroad. Impatient with etiquette, he kept up his usual practice of visiting artisans' and workers' shops, hobnobbing with laborers and soldiers, and eating and drinking to excess.

DEATH OF ALEXIS

Left: the dramatic meeting at Peterhof between Alexis and his father. Below: Castel Sant'Elmo in Naples, where Alexis took refuge. His death gave rise to various rumors: according to some, he had been smothered with pillows; to others, he had been flogged to death; to still others, he had been beheaded. The official version was that he died of a fit upon hearing the death sentence pronounced.

Peter's visit to France marked a turning point in his relations with his son. There had been bitterly tense moments between the two. Peter had given his son a clear ultimatum: either change his ways or take holy orders and be forever excluded from the succession. Alexis at first promised to retire to a monastery, but then changed his mind, saying he would join his father in Copenhagen. Peter waited for him in vain. He eventually learned that the czarevich had first taken refuge in the court of the Holy Roman Emperor in Vienna, then gone on to the Castel Sant'Elmo in Naples.

The grimmest part of this family tragedy now began. Peter dispatched emissaries to Naples, promising Alexis a pardon if he returned home. Alexis was persuaded. At his first meeting with Peter, he threw himself at his father's feet, imploring indulgence. For a brief moment, there seemed to be a reconciliation; but the next day Alexis was called before a high tribunal of noblemen and ecclesiastics. He repeated his confession of guilt and begged to be pardoned. Pardon was granted on condition that he renounce all rights to the succession and make a full confession, naming all of his accomplices. But the czar, determined to be rid

of Alexis once and for all, claimed that Alexis had omitted one detail from his confession: he had not said that while in Vienna he had planned to write a letter to the senators and archbishops to ask for protection from his father. Notes for the letter had been found, and there were witnesses, including Euphrosina, Alexis' mistress, who testified against him. The trial was pure parody. There was not a shred of evidence that Alexis was part of a conspiracy—his "treason" had been no more than the feeble protest of a drunkard making vague, ineffectual motions of revolt. His rebellious thoughts had never led to action. But, since he had confessed them, the outcome was foreordained. He admitted having wanted to see his father dead, to suppress the Petrine reforms, to drive all foreigners from Russian soil, to punish Menshikov. Alexis was seized with convulsions on hearing the death sentence pronounced, and died on June 26, 1718, in the Peter-and-Paul Fortress, following a nocturnal visit from his father. Rumor had it that Peter personally killed him, but no proof of this has ever been unearthed. Before Alexis died, many of his friends and supporters met death on the rack, on the block and under the lash of the knout.

PETER PROCLAIMED "THE GREAT"

The title of Emperor was conferred on Peter by the Senate and Synod following the Treaty of Nystad; his full title became "the Great, Emperor and Father of His Country." It was some time before the title was generally recognized by the chancelleries of the courts of Europe, although it was immediately accepted at home. Years later, only the Poles and the Roman Pope continued not to recognize it. On the whole, Peter had every reason to be pleased. His place in history was assured.

Peter's life at this stage was not all honor and glory: the memory of Alexis' death was still alive, with many insisting that the czarevich had died not of convulsions, but by violence, on his father's orders. Although it is unlikely that Peter killed him with his bare hands, he was entirely capable of it, considering his past. But in that era, Peter's sadism was less unusual: the times, if not more cruel than ours, were at least more frank. Peter's archfoe, Charles XII, for example, treated real or presumed enemies as

harshly as Peter did. Even meek Alexis, taken by his father to witness the torture and execution on the rack of one of his "accomplices," watched an inexpert executioner take three hours to break the victim's bones, without showing the slightest sign of disgust.

Once the Great Northern War with Sweden was ended, and Russia assured an outlet to the sea, Peter turned his attention to the east. The war with Turkey had dealt a stinging blow to his pride and had settled nothing. Peter decided to console himself

by marching on Persia: it appeared a temptingly easy conquest. He found a pretext to act when internal conflict over the succession broke out in Persia in 1722. He moved against Persia with powerful detachments of sailors, bolstered by contingents of Tatars and Kalmucks. Defeating the minor potentates he encountered on his way, Peter overpowered the sultan and went on to Baku. The peace treaty, signed in 1723, assured him possession of all the territory he had seized by force of arms.

RUSSIA BECOMES A BALTIC POWER

Below, from top to bottom: the fortress of Kronstad, which Peter built to bar land and sea access to St. Petersburg; naval encounter between the Russians and Swedes (July 27, 1720); view of the city of Reval in Livonia. Reval (Tallinn) was taken by the Russians in 1710 and was ceded to them by Sweden in 1721.

Opposite page, bottom, from left to right: three engravings showing concluding phases of the Great Northern War: Livonian peasants being flogged; the arrival of captured ships at St. Petersburg (Peter appears in the boat in the foreground); fireworks celebrating the peace between Russia and Sweden. In the large engraving: the great naval battle of Hangud in 1714, in which the Russians defeated the Swedes.

One of Peter's greatest wishes was to have a southern, warm-water outlet to the sea, but Turkey steadfastly prevented it. Forced to make do with what he had, he concentrated on turning the Baltic into a Russian lake. For this reason, among others, the czar was especially fond of St. Petersburg. His house there was similar to the one in Preobrazhensk: four little rooms with doorways so low that he had to stoop when passing from room to room. It was here that he worked out his most daring and ambitious plans, here that new Petrine reforms took shape. If at first Peter stressed superficial changes—which were nonetheless substantial in a society as rigid as old Russia's—he now aimed at giving Russia a new order, at turning her into a modern country in spirit as well as in appearance.

The second stage of the Petrine reforms was initiated after the end of the Great Northern War. The war, which lasted for 21 years, had thrown together men of all classes in extraordinary circumstances: thus it provided the first impulse for change. Like the building of St. Petersburg, it had required money; and Peter, forced to take money wherever he could find it, ended by destroying the old central administration. He divided Russia into eight governing regions, each region being made up of provinces, which were in turn subdivided into districts. Each governing region was assigned a general, to whom the czar allocated funds. In exchange, the regions had to raise and pay for the maintenance of a certain number of regiments. The first division of Russia into provinces took place between 1710 and 1712. The capital was moved to St. Petersburg; the czar surrounded himself with foreign advisers and tried to take further steps forward. He created, along Swedish lines, three collegial bodies to deal with fiscal administration, together with another three aimed at increasing overall national output. Completing this reorganization, and functioning above the "colleges," which had roughly the status of federal departments, was a senate, the supreme juridical and administrative body. And at the top of the pyramid stood the czar, Peter the Great.

Below: an engraving of 1717, showing the palace at Peterhof. Right, below: the River Neva and St. Petersburg; above: buildings along the Neva in present-day Leningrad Russia's "window onto Europe" had a great influence on the development of Russian literature.

One of the most celebrated works of poetry treating St. Petersburg and its origins is by the great Polish poet Adam Mickiewicz who, in his epic poem Forefathers, *was struck by the czar's force of will in building the city; the poet entirely overlooked the political reasons for Peter's choice of the site. But the origins of the myth of St. Petersburg are found chiefly in Pushkin's* Bronze Cavalier; *Pushkin was entranced, a century after Peter, by the beauty of this city the czar had founded.*

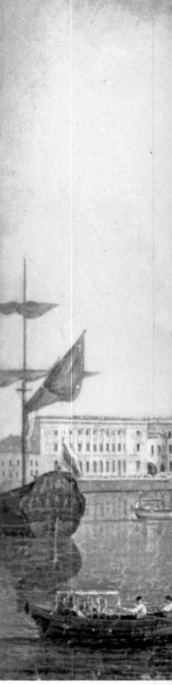

St. Petersburg created many problems for its founder. Although it was intended to bring Russia to the sea, English and Dutch merchantmen continued to make greater use of Archangel; this was because St. Petersburg itself could not be reached by river, and exports, mostly hemp, required almost prohibitive transportation costs. Peter had canals dug and depots built; finally, in 1715, he simply forbade the sale of hemp anywhere else. Maritime trade immediately increased. But there were other problems: the water, which was extremely salty, corroded the ships' planks; and the canals were so shallow that it was hard to bring in lumber. Meanwhile, Peter's city grew more and more beautiful and imposing. Artists and artisans of many nationalities, especially French, were at work there. In November, 1715, Zotov, an emissary of the czar, journeyed to Paris to enlist the best craftsmen France had to offer. In 1716 Lefort succeeded in sending to Russia a sizable contingent of artists, led by the architect Leblond. He brought with him a draftsman, Nicolas Girard, and the hydraulic engineer Gerard Sualem. Another group of artists was led by the sculptor Nicolas Pineau.

After forcing the Russian nobility to build homes in the new capital, Peter set up the new state bureaucracy. Formerly, the great landed estates of the nobility had been of two types—either patrimonial and hereditary, or derived from a government office; both systems were losing strength when Peter arrived on the scene and abolished them entirely. In 1722 he established, instead, a Table of Ranks, composed of 14 classes in which the entire nobility was rigidly pigeon-holed. All were obligated to serve the czar in either the civil administration or the military. In short, every nobleman was given a rank and a uniform. The reform was of the greatest importance: it meant that the czar's officers were no longer officers because they were noblemen, but rather were noblemen because they were officers. The distinction was greater than might be supposed.

A WINDOW ONTO EUROPE

Alexandre Leblond played a leading role in the building of St. Petersburg. Given the title of Architect-General, which meant that he enjoyed absolute authority over all the architects working there, he had free lodgings and drew a salary of 5,000 rubles a year, which, for the times, was considerable. One of the terms of his contract obliged him to teach his art to young Russian architects, concealing none of his secrets. Leblond set to work in the face of innumerable obstacles, not the least being the hostility of Peter's favorite, Menshikov, the patron of another architect. Menshikov was not a man to be troubled by scruples or even to shrink from sabotage: it was partly his fault that St. Petersburg, at one stage, suffered from a serious flood caused by the shallowness of the canals. Obviously, in an atmosphere of jealousy, rivalry and envy, there was no end of plotting and intrigue.

Few of Peter's achievements remain as admirable as his "window onto Europe." The legend is perhaps more glorious than the fact. Still, with St. Petersburg, the czar did create something revolutionary, destroying all links with tradition. St. Petersburg was not a city of the people. It was built for an exclusive group: the first Russian cosmopolitan aristocracy. The palaces of St. Petersburg, the paintings and sculptures of the new city, belonged to a world vastly different from that of ancient Moscow. It is altogether understandable that among Alexis' projects was the restoration of Moscow as first city of the nation. St. Petersburg, for Alexis and the monks who backed him, was a symbol of evil. But Catherine the Great, who inherited and carried on Peter's work, consolidated the authority of St. Petersburg, which was to last until the Revolution of 1917.

Opposite page, top: the
Peter-and-Paul Fortress,
seen from the River Neva;
below, left: a palace on
the Neva. Below: cupolas
of the Church of the Savior.
These three views of Leningrad
today are imposing evidence
of the impress left by
Peter the Great. St. Petersburg
arose from a wasteland:
even wildlife was brought in
where there had previously
been none, as is seen in the
engraving on the opposite page,
showing various types of
hunting. Around Moscow
small game, especially birds,
were trapped alive. Peter had
thousands of songbirds transferred
from the Moscow countryside
and woods to St. Petersburg,
where the only wildlife consisted
primarily of ferocious wolves.

DEATH OF PETER

Left: Peter on his deathbed. The last rites were administered to him by the Bishop of Pskov. Center: the czar leaving the throne to his wife. Before dying, Peter tried to write something, but got no farther than "Give everything . . ." He left no will, and the document long believed by some to be his political testament is today considered apocryphal. Popular sentiment on Peter's death is marvelously expressed in the woodprint on the right, entitled, "The Mice Bury a Cat." The cat, of course, is Peter, and the mice are his subjects, freed by his death from a nightmare.

Few people managed to remain close to Peter throughout his lifetime, or to enjoy his lasting favor. Peter was a man who consumed, like a flame, all who served or loved him, colleagues and mistresses alike. But Catherine proved resistant and durable. More than he needed her, and he did need her, the czar admired her for her iron character and keen intelligence. Catherine gave evidence of her character on many occasions. It once nearly cost her her life.

Just a month before her coronation as empress, Peter discovered that she had a lover, a handsome, amiable young man, the brother, as it happened, of Anna Mons, the czar's old favorite. Peter had him arrested and put to death; he then brought Catherine to the gallows. Catherine betrayed not the slightest emotion. That evening Peter had the young man's head placed in a tankard of spirits and set upon the mantelpiece. Still Catherine showed no emotion. In a fit of rage, Peter smashed a precious Venetian mirror: Catherine calmly remarked that he had broken one of the loveliest ornaments in their home. It was in the hands of a person of such character that Peter determined to leave the succession; more than that, in the hands of one who would

70

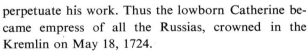

perpetuate his work. Thus the lowborn Catherine became empress of all the Russias, crowned in the Kremlin on May 18, 1724.

Peter's life was fast running out. His extraordinary constitution, weakened by a life of excesses, began to give way; he was suffering from kidney stones and the aftereffects of a venereal disease. Exhausted from an arduous inspection trip to the latest of his huge public works, the canal at Lake Ladoga, he returned to St. Petersburg in the autumn of 1724. On Twelfth Night he caught a cold participating in the traditional ceremony of the Blessing of the Waters on the Neva. Suffering from violent kidney pains, Peter took to his bed; several days later, on January 28, 1725, he died.

There were not many who wept at his passing; many, in fact, breathed a sigh of relief—the tyrant was dead. For many others, Peter had been Antichrist, an incarnation of the devil.

Popular rumor had it that he died from a dose of poison administered by Catherine, in revenge for the suffering of her young lover. This story appears quite as fanciful as so many others of this period. In any case,

Catherine, the former servant girl, ascended the throne.

Peter was not quite 53 when he died. He had not spared himself. Nature had endowed him with exceptional strength, vigorous health and prodigious nervous energy. The liberal education he had received, or rather had taken, had contributed to strengthening his character and will. Speaking of him, Princess Sophia of Hanover remarked, "He must be very good and very wicked," which was a judgment both acute and exact in its apparent simplicity. Peter was capable of generous impulses and moments of heartfelt goodness, but he also possessed a streak of fierce cruelty, abundantly evident on such occasions as the several massacres of the *strieltsy*, the murder of his son, and the unspeakable tortures inflicted on his enemies and adversaries. He often had fine flashes of intuition; but he seemed not to know when to stop or how to pause and reflect. He followed the call of impulse: many of the Petrine reforms, wholly justified by subsequent events, were conceived in haste and executed with impatience. Nothing was so alien to his spirit as the desire for advice or approval. He did not understand men's feelings, nor did he want to.

THE PRICE OF REFORM

Among the greatest weaknesses of Peter's reign was his failure to create a ruling class that would survive him. Many of his reforms, even some of the better ones, were abolished or allowed to lapse because few men were willing to continue Peter's work. Like all despots, Peter did not want colleagues, but servants: he appreciated his associates only insofar as they were slavishly obedient. His strong will and keen, inquisitive mind made him want to accomplish everything at once. He did not lack sensitivity, but the violence of his temperament frequently led him to do things whose long-range effects he could not immediately judge. He despised Russian traditionalism, but was unable accurately to judge its strength. Measures like the prohibition of beards and the shortening of clothes were useless and provocative acts; meant to be shortcuts to modernity, in the end they only lengthened the process by fostering discontent, rancor and resistance. Peter imposed himself on Russia, but it never accepted him wholeheartedly. The populace was decidedly hostile to him, and the Old Ritualists had no trouble depicting him as Antichrist. He did not bother to explain his behavior, to make his decisions in any way comprehensible.

There is no denying the importance of the modernization of Russia, which he carried out in a very brief span of time. Peter the reformer left a lasting impress on every aspect of Russian culture and customs. The reform of the calendar and of the alphabet; the stimulus to science and the arts; the establishment of schools, and the spreading of basic education to broad strata of the general population; the liberation of women from centuries of inferiority; the reform of the church and reduction of its role in secular life; the struggle against superstition; the tolerance of foreign religions; the creation of a navy and administrative and military reforms; the stimulus to the evolution of customs and social life—here the Petrine reforms proved crucial, worthwhile and lasting.

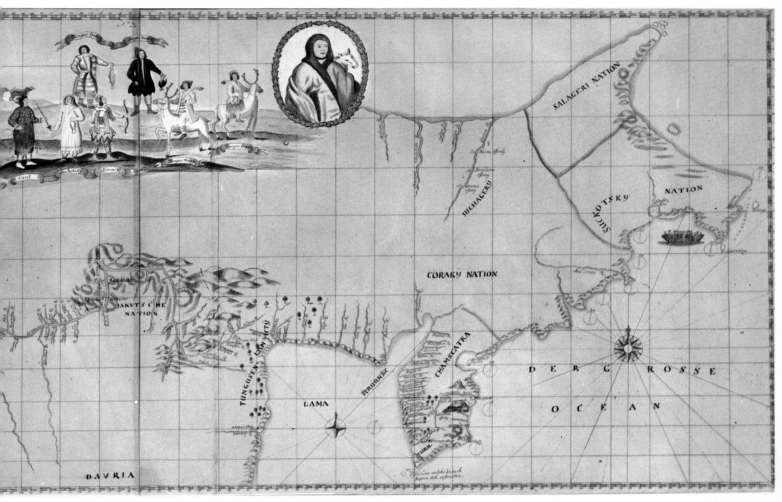

To the last, Peter dreamed of a Russia on the open sea. Three weeks before his death he wrote instructions for Captain Vitus Bering, a Dane serving in the Russian navy, charging him with finding out whether Asia and North America were separated by the sea. Only in 1728 did the explorer find out what the czar had wanted to know, when he discovered the strait and sea that bear his name. The map (above), which dates from 1729, shows the route taken by the expedition. Below, far left: two peasants in traditional costumes on the peninsula of Kamchatka (Chamscatka on the map), where Bering founded Petropavlovsk-Kamchatskii. Left: an idealized portrait of Peter the Great, in an engraving of the period.

"*He stripped away the mysterious cloak in which the person of the czar had been wrapped,*" wrote Alexander Herzen in his Short History of the Russians, "*and cast off the Byzantine cowl worn by his predecessors,*" appearing before his subjects as "*a simple mortal.*" *The bronze bust by Bartolomeo Carlo Rastrelli nicely catches the human side of Peter, a mixture of intelligence, candor, inflexibility and determination. Herzen called Peter "an imperial revolutionary." Perhaps the most appealing and fascinating side of his character was his capacity to behave like the most ordinary of his subjects.*

1672—May 30: birth of Peter, in Moscow, to Czar Alexis Mikhailovich Romanov and his second wife, Natalia Kirilovna Naryshkina. June 29: baptized Peter after the saint of the day, according to Russian Orthodox custom.

1676—Death of Czar Alexis.

1676–82—Reign of Fedor, Peter's half-brother, son of his father's first wife.

1682—May: revolt of the *strieltsy* (palace guard and backbone of the army, instituted by Ivan the Terrible).

1682–89—Regency of Sophia on behalf of Ivan V and Peter. Peter and his mother withdraw to Preobrazhensk, where the child spends his time at war games.

1683—September 12: Jan Sobieski, King of Poland, defeats the Turks, who have laid siege to Vienna. The decline of the Ottoman Empire begins.

1689—January: Peter marries Eudoxia Lopukhina. He confines his half-sister Sophia, guilty of conspiring against him, in the Convent of Novodevich.

1690—February 19: birth of the Czarevich Alexis.

1693—Peter visits Archangel; here, realizing the importance of the sea to Russia, he takes the first steps for building a fleet.

1696—January 29: death of Ivan V; Peter rules alone. July: at first unsuccessful, the army and the new fleet take Azov from the Turks.

1697—Traveling as Peter Mikhailov at the head of a large caravan, he embarks on a long journey to Western Europe. Charles XII, just turned 15, is crowned King of Sweden.

1698—August: Peter sets out hurriedly for home on hearing of a new revolt of the *strieltsy*. In Poland, however, he learns that the revolt has been put down and stays to make the acquaintance of Augustus II.

1699—Secret pact between Peter and Augustus II against Sweden.

1700—Westernization of clothes and reform of the calendar (1700 from the birth of Christ replaces 7028 from the Creation); simplification of the alphabet. The Russian army is defeated at Narva by Charles XII of Sweden.

1701–02—The Russians occupy Livonia and Estonia.

1703—January 2: publication of the first issue of the first Russian newspaper, *Vedomosti* (*News*). May 29: founding of St. Petersburg.

1709—June 27 (Julian calendar) or July 8 (Gregorian calendar): the Russians defeat the Swedes at Poltava, returning Augustus to the Polish throne which had been occupied by Stanislas Leczynski after the Swedish victory at Narva.

1711—The Pruth campaign, in Bessarabia, ends in disaster; Peter opens negotiations with the Turks, to whom he is forced to return Azov. October: marriage of Czarevich Alexis and Princess Sophia-Charlotte of Brunswick-Wölfenbüttel. Birth of the writer and scientist Michael V. Lomonosov.

1712—March 12: Peter officially marries Martha Skavronskaia, later to become the Empress Catherine I.

1713—The capital is moved from Moscow to St. Petersburg.

1713–15—The Russian army and fleet seize Finland (which is later returned to Sweden following the Treaty of Nystad).

1715—Czarevich Alexis' wife dies during childbirth, leaving a son, who is later to reign as Peter II.

1716—Bitter disagreements between Peter and his son lead Alexis to take refuge abroad.

1717—Peter journeys to Paris, where he proposes a Franco-Russian alliance, but obtains only a promise of neutrality.

1718—Despite promises made beforehand, Alexis is put on trial. June 26: death of Czarevich Alexis in prison. Charles XII of Sweden dies fighting the Danes.

1720—Russian naval victories over Sweden.

1721—September 10: following a series of separate peace treaties, the Treaty of Nystad brings an end to the Great Northern War. The Russian patriarchy is abolished; the Church is placed under the Holy Synod, answering directly to the sovereign. Peter I is proclaimed Peter the Great, Emperor of Russia and Father of his Country.

1722—War with Persia.

1723—Peter the Great conquers the western banks of the Caspian Sea and occupies Baku.

1724—May 18: Peter's second wife, Catherine, is crowned empress.

1725—January 28: the czar dies in St. Petersburg. He is succeeded, for two years, by his widow, Empress Catherine I.